ANIMALS OF THE CORAL REEF

Sea Snakes

WITHDRAWN

by Lindsay Shaffer

BELLWETHER MEDIA • MINNEAPOLIS, MN

Note to Librarians, Teachers, and Parents:

Blastoff! Readers are carefully developed by literacy experts and combine standards-based content with developmentally appropriate text.

Level 1 provides the most support through repetition of high-frequency words, light text, predictable sentence patterns, and strong visual support.

Level 2 offers early readers a bit more challenge through varied simple sentences, increased text load, and less repetition of high-frequency words.

Level 3 advances early-fluent readers toward fluency through increased text and concept load, less reliance on visuals, longer sentences, and more literary language.

Level 4 builds reading stamina by providing more text per page, increased use of punctuation, greater variation in sentence patterns, and increasingly challenging vocabulary.

Level 5 encourages children to move from "learning to read" to "reading to learn" by providing even more text, varied writing styles, and less familiar topics.

Whichever book is right for your reader, Blastoff! Readers are the perfect books to build confidence and encourage a love of reading that will last a lifetime!

This edition first published in 2020 by Bellwether Media, Inc.

No part of this publication may be reproduced in whole or in part without written permission of the publisher. For information regarding permission, write to Bellwether Media, Inc., Attention: Permissions Department, 6012 Blue Circle Drive, Minnetonka, MN 55343.

Library of Congress Cataloging-in-Publication Data

Names: Shaffer, Lindsay, author.
Title: Sea Snakes / by Lindsay Shaffer.
Description: Minneapolis, MN : Bellwether Media, Inc., 2020. | Series: Animals of the coral reef | Includes bibliographical references and index. | Audience: Ages 5-8 | Audience: Grades K-1 | Summary: "Relevant images match informative text in this introduction to sea snakes. Intended for students in kindergarten through third grade"-- Provided by publisher.
Identifiers: LCCN 2019033059 (print) | LCCN 2019033060 (ebook) | ISBN 9781644871348 (library binding) | ISBN 9781618918161 (ebook)
Subjects: LCSH: Sea snakes--Juvenile literature.
Classification: LCC QL666.O64 S53 2020 (print) | LCC QL666.O64 (ebook) |DDC 597.96/5--dc23
LC record available at https://lccn.loc.gov/2019033059
LC ebook record available at https://lccn.loc.gov/2019033060

Text copyright © 2020 by Bellwether Media, Inc. BLASTOFF! READERS and associated logos are trademarks and/or registered trademarks of Bellwether Media, Inc.

Editor: Betsy Rathburn   Designer: Laura Sowers

Printed in the United States of America, North Mankato, MN.

Table of Contents

Life in the Coral Reef	4
Staying Fresh	12
Open Wide!	16
Glossary	22
To Learn More	23
Index	24

Life in the Coral Reef

faint-banded sea snake

Sea snakes are **venomous** ocean **reptiles**. They live in warm oceans around the world.

Some sea snakes are **kraits**. Many live in the coral reef **biome**.

Faint-banded Sea Snake Range

range =

Sea snakes are at home underwater. They use their flat tails like paddles.

olive sea snake

yellow-lipped sea krait

Their long, thin bodies help them swim fast!

Sea snakes have **adapted** to the salty water of coral reefs.

banded sea krait

Special Adaptations

flat tail

long, thin body

salt gland

They have special **glands** near their tongues. These help them spit out extra salt!

Sea snakes go to the surface to breathe. But they can also breathe through their skin.

This gives them enough air for long dives. They can stay under for three hours!

11

Staying Fresh

Ocean water is too salty to drink. Sea snakes must find freshwater.

The snakes likely go to the surface to drink rainwater!

Faint-banded Sea Snake Stats

Least Concern	Near Threatened	Vulnerable	Endangered	Critically Endangered	Extinct in the Wild	Extinct

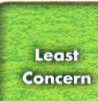

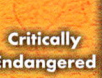

conservation status: least concern

life span: up to 10 years

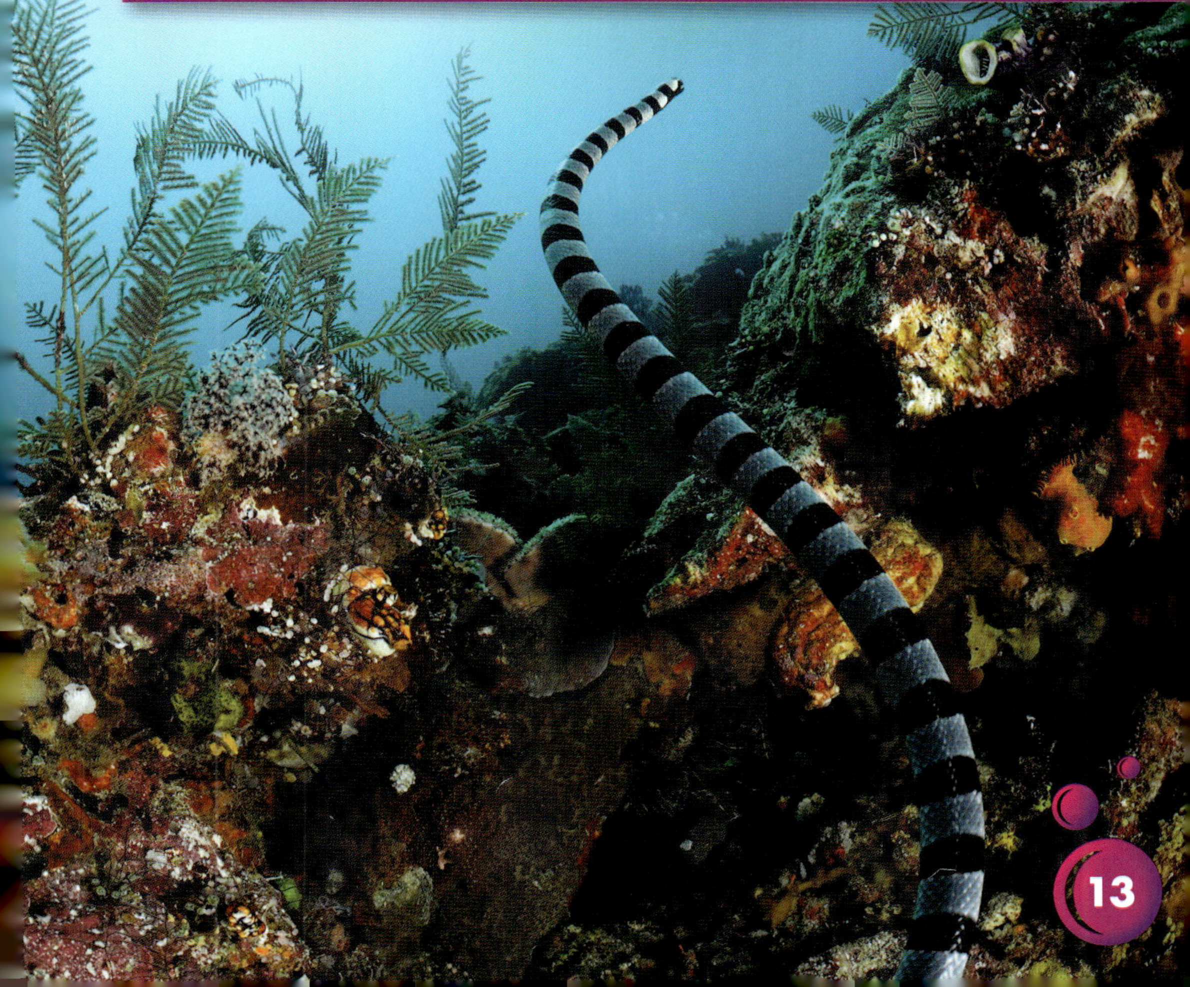

Coral reefs are full of **algae** and **barnacles**. These may attach to sea snakes.

shedding skin

The snakes must **shed** their skin to get rid of them!

Open Wide!

Sea snakes are **carnivores**. They feast on eels, fish eggs, and **mollusks**.

Their jaws open wide to swallow **prey** in one bite!

Sea snakes search for prey near reefs. They poke their heads into cracks.

Sea Snake Diet

green moray eels

prawns

fish eggs

When they spot prey, sea snakes bite. They release their venom!

Sea snakes gobble up their weakened prey.

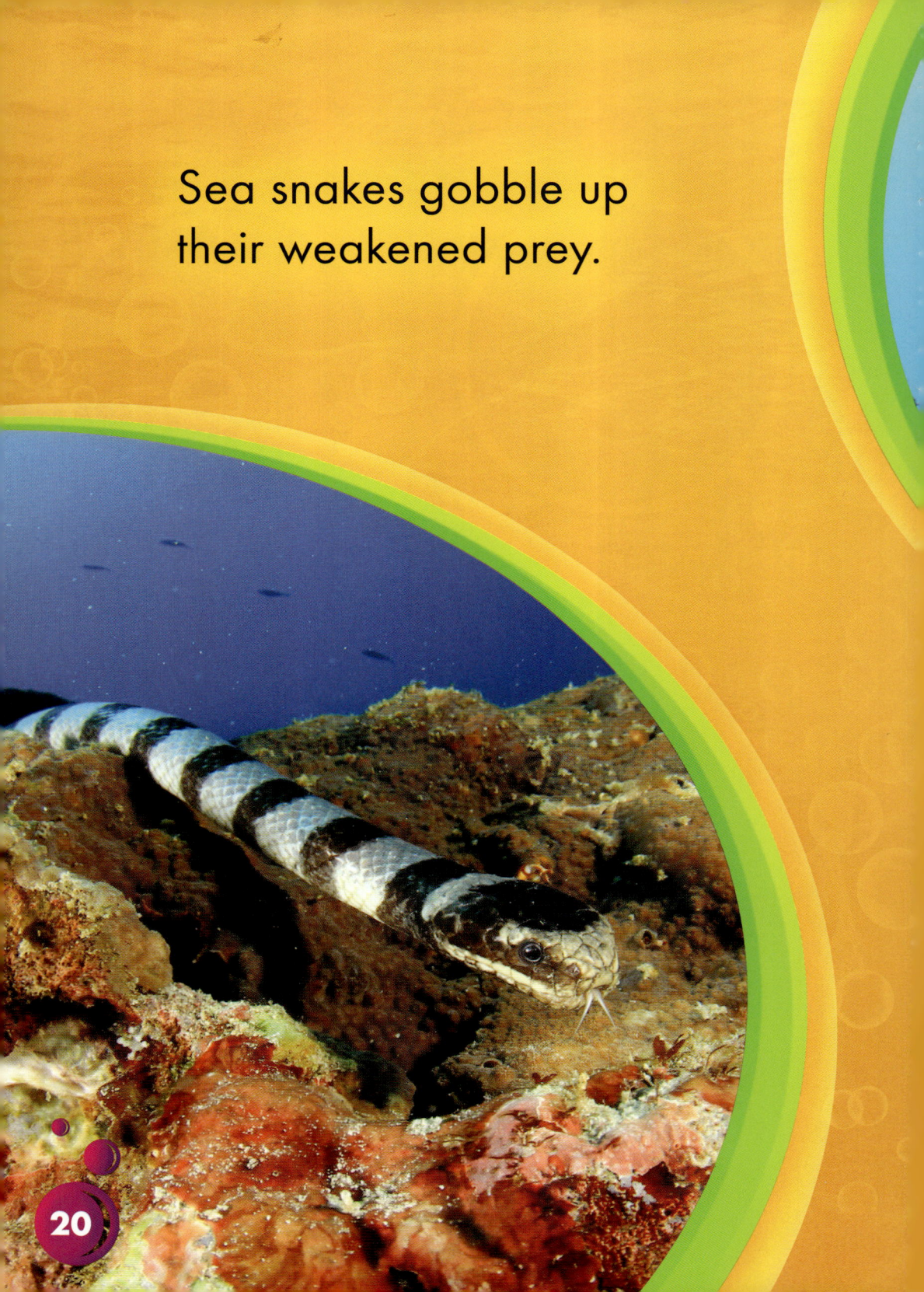

These **predators** find plenty of food in the coral reef biome!

Glossary

adapted—changed to fit different conditions

algae—plants and plantlike living things; most kinds of algae grow in water.

barnacles—hard-shelled water animals that attach themselves to surfaces

biome—a large area with certain plants, animals, and weather

carnivores—animals that only eat meat

glands—body parts that add or remove something from the body; sea snakes have glands that remove salt from the body.

kraits—a type of snake that has bold stripes and is active at night

mollusks—animals with no backbones such as snails, octopuses, and squids; mollusks usually have hard shells.

predators—animals that hunt other animals for food

prey—animals that are hunted by other animals for food

reptiles—cold-blooded animals that have backbones and lay eggs

shed—to lose something on the body; sea snakes shed their skin.

venomous—able to produce a poison called venom

To Learn More

AT THE LIBRARY

Black, Vanessa. *Sea Snakes*. Minneapolis, Minn.: Bullfrog Books, 2017.

George, Gale. *Sea Snakes*. New York, N.Y.: PowerKids Press, 2016.

Hulick, Kathryn. *Coral Reefs*. New York, N.Y.: AV2 by Weigl, 2019.

ON THE WEB

FACTSURFER

Factsurfer.com gives you a safe, fun way to find more information.

1. Go to www.factsurfer.com.
2. Enter "sea snakes" into the search box and click .
3. Select your book cover to see a list of related web sites.

Index

adaptations, 8, 9
algae, 14
barnacles, 14
biome, 5, 21
bite, 17, 19
bodies, 7, 9
breathe, 10
carnivores, 16
dives, 11
drink, 12
food, 16, 19, 21
glands, 9
jaws, 17
kraits, 5
oceans, 4, 12
predators, 21
prey, 16, 17, 18, 19, 20
range, 4, 5
reptiles, 4

salt, 8, 9, 12
shed, 15
skin, 10, 15
status, 13
surface, 10, 12
swim, 7
tails, 6, 9
tongues, 9
venomous, 4, 19
water, 6, 8, 12

The images in this book are reproduced through the courtesy of: Rich Carey, front cover (sea snake), pp. 14-15, 20, 22; John_Walker, front cover (coral reef), pp. 2-3; Nature Picture Library/ Alamy, pp. 4-5, 12-13; Brandon Cole Marine Photography/ Alamy, p. 6; Ethan Daniels, pp. 6-7, 9, 19 (eels); Krzysztof Bargiel, p. 8; tswinner, p. 11; John Cuyos, p. 12; Linda Pitkin, p. 15; marinuse - Underwater/ Alamy, pp. 16-17; tae208, p. 18; Podolnaya Elena, p. 19 (prawns); scubaluna, p. 19 (fish eggs); elena_photo_sou, pp. 20-21.